HOW TO DRAW
MAGICAL KINGS AND QUEENS

Steve Beaumont

PowerKiDS
press.
New York

Published in 2008 by The Rosen Publishing Group, Inc.
29 East 21st Street, New York, NY 10010

Artwork and text: Steve Beaumont
Editor (Arcturus): Alex Woolf
Editor (Rosen): Jennifer Way
Designer: Jane Hawkins

Library of Congress Cataloging-in-Publication Data

Beaumont, Steve.
  How to draw magical kings and queens / Steve Beaumont.
      p. cm. — (Drawing fantasy art)
  Includes index.
  ISBN-13: 978-1-4042-3860-2 (library binding)
  ISBN-10: 1-4042-3860-3 (libray binding)
  1. Kings and rulers in art—Juvenile literature. 2. Queens in art—
Juvenile literature. 3. Fantasy in art—Juvenile literature. 4. Drawing—
Technique—Juvenile literature. I. Title.
  NC825.K52B43 2008
  743.4—dc22

                                2007001600

Printed in China

Contents

Introduction

The characters in fantasy books, movies, and games come in many forms, from magical heroes to evil villains. Have you ever thought that it might be fun to create your own, original characters? If so, this is the book for you! It will teach you how to draw the rulers of the fantasy realm, fairy-tale kings and queens.

When you draw fantasy characters, you are the boss! Fairy-tale kings, queens, and creatures are products of your imagination, which means that you do not have to follow too many rules. It is important to pay attention to the basic rules of anatomy and perspective, but the rest is up to you. Get creative! Make your characters as wild and original as you want.

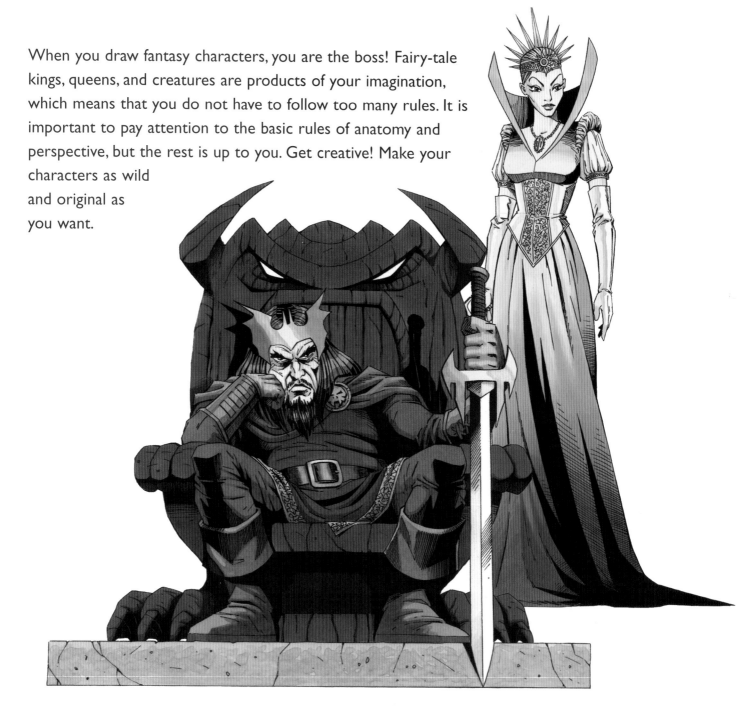

Kings

He is ruler of his land and ruler of his people. The weight of such responsibility could only be carried on the shoulders of a great man. In the days when kingdoms regularly waged war on each other, a king's people needed to feel safe and secure in the knowledge that their ruler was brave of heart and fierce of sword, a big man with a big heart. Unfortunately, power can sometimes corrupt a man's heart and mind, creating evil kings who oppress their people and rule only for themselves.

Queens

In sword and sorcery, the responsibility of leadership does not always fall on the shoulders of male characters. Many kingdoms are ruled, and many a battle has been won, by a strong-minded woman with an iron will. As with kings, there are both good and evil queens, and in this book you will encounter both extremes.

Equipment

Before you begin, you need to gather high-quality materials and equipment. Good tools will help you create good illustrations.

Paper

Cheap paper is fine for your practice sketches. When you progress to ink drawing, use line art paper, which you can find in most art stores.

Watercolor paints look best on watercolor paper. Different weights and sizes of this paper will give you different results.

Pencils

There are many different types of pencils, and it is a good idea to have a few. Hard-lead pencils are long lasting and will not smudge much. Soft-lead pencils are darker and quick to wear down. If you are just starting out, a number 4 pencil is a good choice.

When you are working on the details in your illustration, choose a mechanical pencil. Mechanical pencils come in a range of lead thicknesses, but 0.5 mm is a good size with which to start.

Pens

Use a ballpoint or a simple dip pen and nib when you are inking. Use a felt-tip pen for coloring. Most art stores carry a variety of felt-tips.

Markers

Markers can give great results if you know how to use them. Practice will help you get the look you want.

Brushes

It is more difficult to use a fine brush for inking line work than it is to use a pen, but it can be worth it. If you want to practice brushwork, buy some good-quality sable brushes. They will give you the best results.

Watercolors and gouache

Go to your local art shop to find a wide range of these products, from student to professional quality.

Inks

Any good brand of ink will work.

Eraser

Why not give all three types of erasers a try? You can choose from rubber, plastic, or putty.

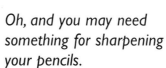

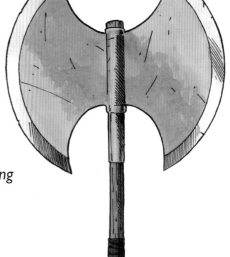

Oh, and you may need something for sharpening your pencils.

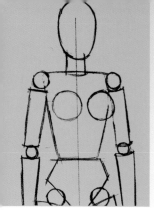

Basic Construction

Before we start on some projects, let's look at an easy way of constructing human figures. In fantasy illustration, all characters can be broken down into geometric shapes.

Anyone who can hold a pencil can draw two-dimensional geometric shapes such as squares, triangles, and circles. However, these shapes on their own will not make your characters seem real. If you can draw three-dimensional shapes such as cylinders, cubes, spheres, and egg shapes, it will help give form and solidity to your characters. Here are some examples.

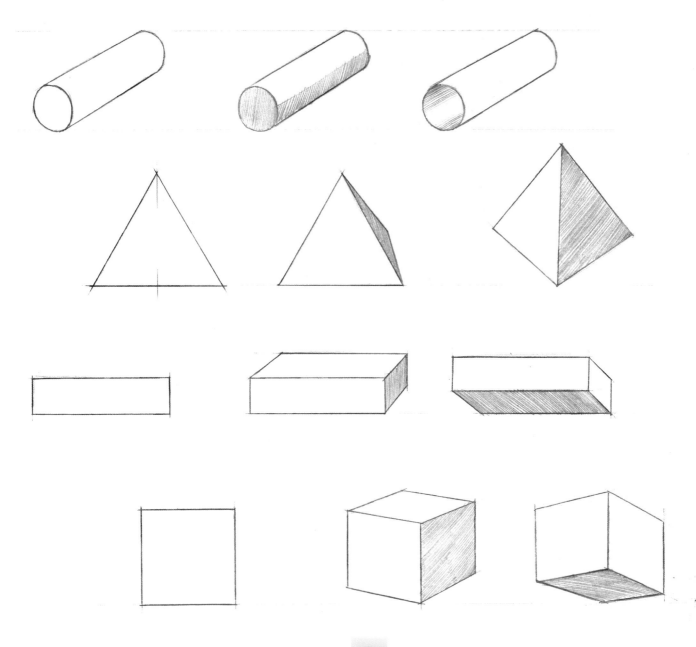

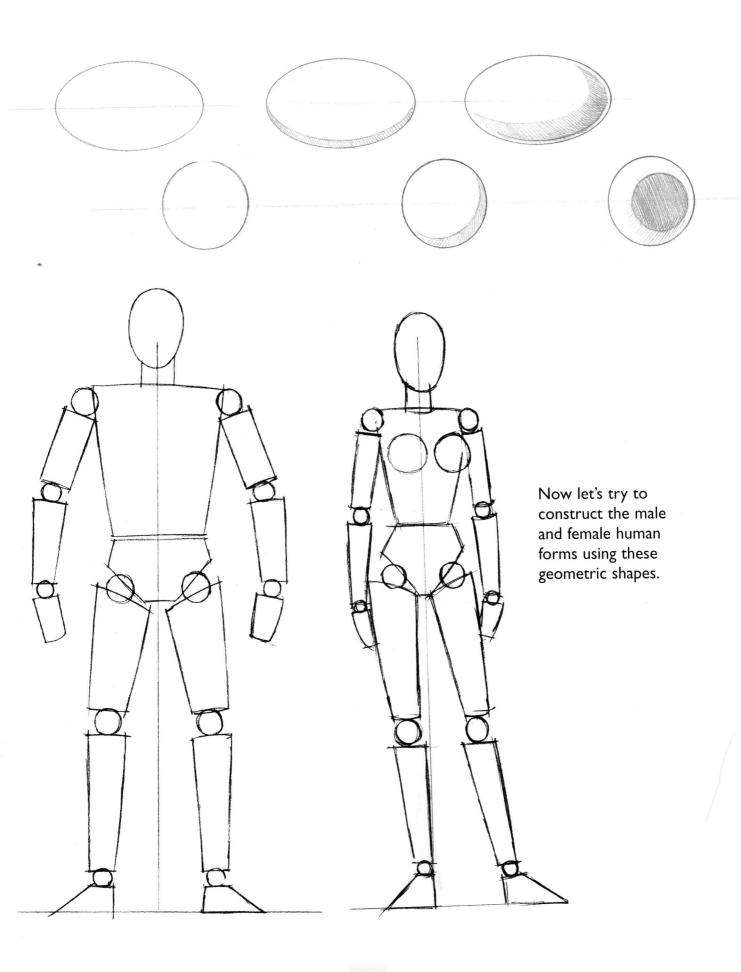

Now let's try to construct the male and female human forms using these geometric shapes.

Good King

The pose we have chosen for this king suggests that, although he is mighty, he uses his power wisely. Respected by his subjects and feared by his enemies, he is the type of king who thinks before he acts. If he is attacked, though, he will not hesitate to raise his heavy sword.

Stage 1
Start with a stick figure to establish the basic shape. Construct a solid, royal pose.

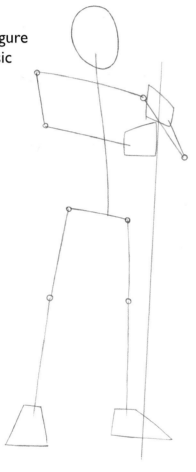

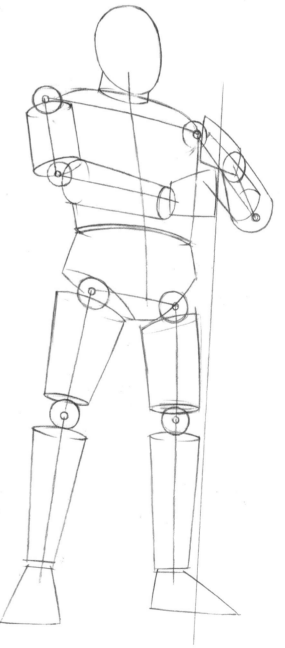

Stage 2
Now add geometric shapes to give some form to his chest and limbs (see pages 8–9).

Stage 3

Now add the outer body form and the facial features. Try practicing different facial expressions before applying one to your drawing. The king's face should show his strength of character. Add a bushy beard to complete it.

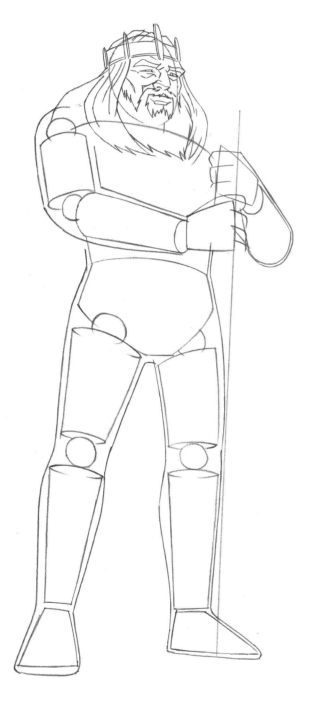

Stage 4

This is not the type of king to dress in rich, fancy clothing. His clothes will be of the finest material but they will also be functional enough for battle. Give him heavy-duty leather breastplates, gloves, boots, and a heavy broadsword. Place a cloak around his shoulders.

Stage 5
Add details to his hair and armor and add some shading to give definition to his overall form.

Stage 6
Start to apply ink to the figure.

Stage 7
Note how the use of solid areas of black ink gives strength to this drawing.

Stage 8

You can color your drawing, if you like, using marker pens, felt-tips, or watercolors. Lay down each color in one continuous wash if you can, applying the color as smoothly as possible. The colors that suit this king are rich, warm browns and reds.

Evil King

This king, who probably obtained his crown by foul play, wants only power and riches. He is spiteful and forever suspicious of plots against him. There is no brave heart here, just a black one, twisted and cruel.

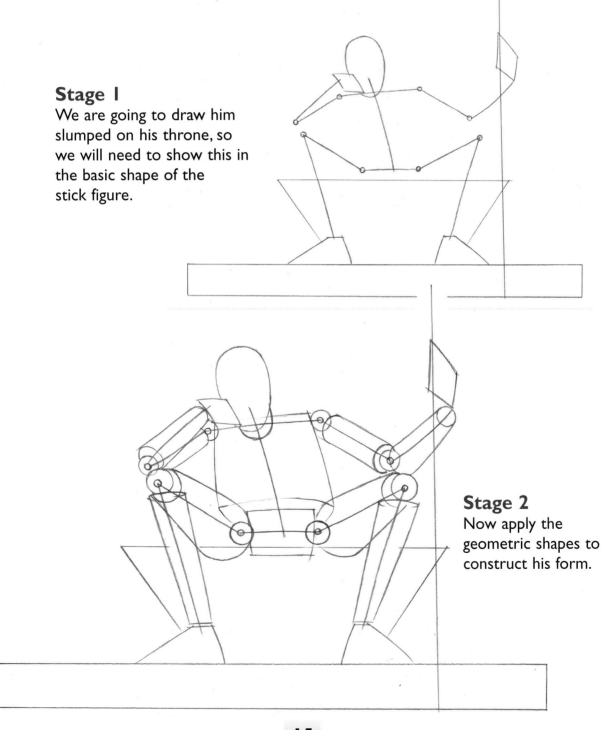

Stage 1
We are going to draw him slumped on his throne, so we will need to show this in the basic shape of the stick figure.

Stage 2
Now apply the geometric shapes to construct his form.

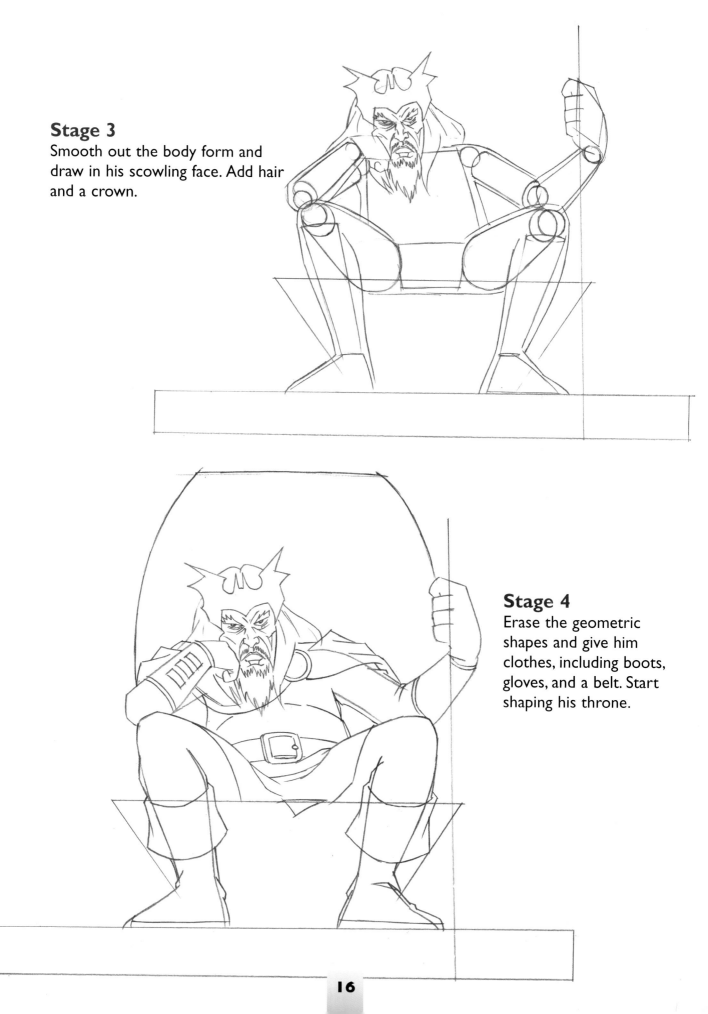

Stage 3
Smooth out the body form and draw in his scowling face. Add hair and a crown.

Stage 4
Erase the geometric shapes and give him clothes, including boots, gloves, and a belt. Start shaping his throne.

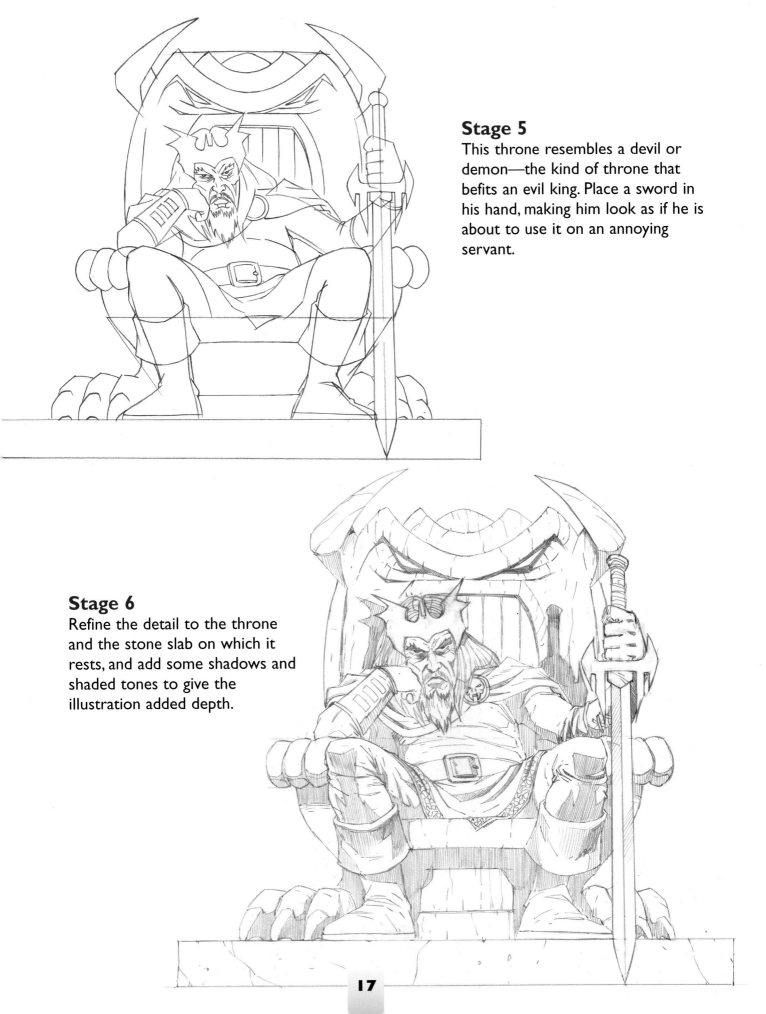

Stage 5

This throne resembles a devil or demon—the kind of throne that befits an evil king. Place a sword in his hand, making him look as if he is about to use it on an annoying servant.

Stage 6

Refine the detail to the throne and the stone slab on which it rests, and add some shadows and shaded tones to give the illustration added depth.

Stage 7
Start to ink in the drawing.

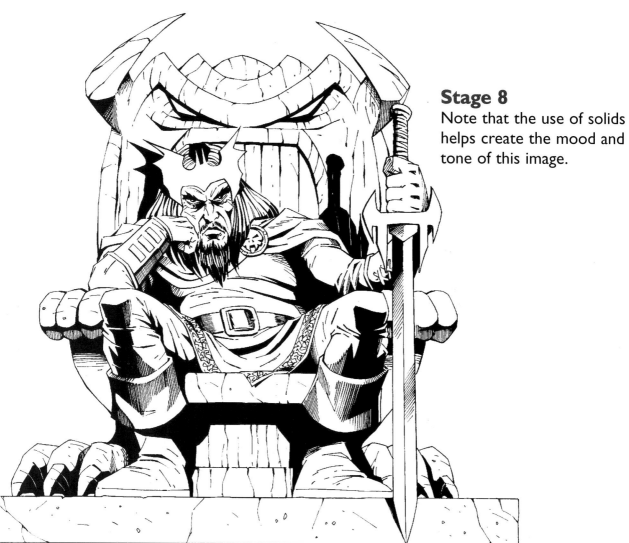

Stage 8
Note that the use of solids helps create the mood and tone of this image.

Stage 9

Since this character is consumed by evil, it may seem like a good idea to seat him on a black throne. Although this would look cool, it would not help display the king very well. So, to add some contrast, we will show the throne as a heavy wood construction.

Good Queen

Although this queen seems to be a young woman, she has a wise head on her shoulders and rules with kindness and fairness. A fantasy character's looks do not always tell the whole story. Often those who appear young are actually wise beyond their years.

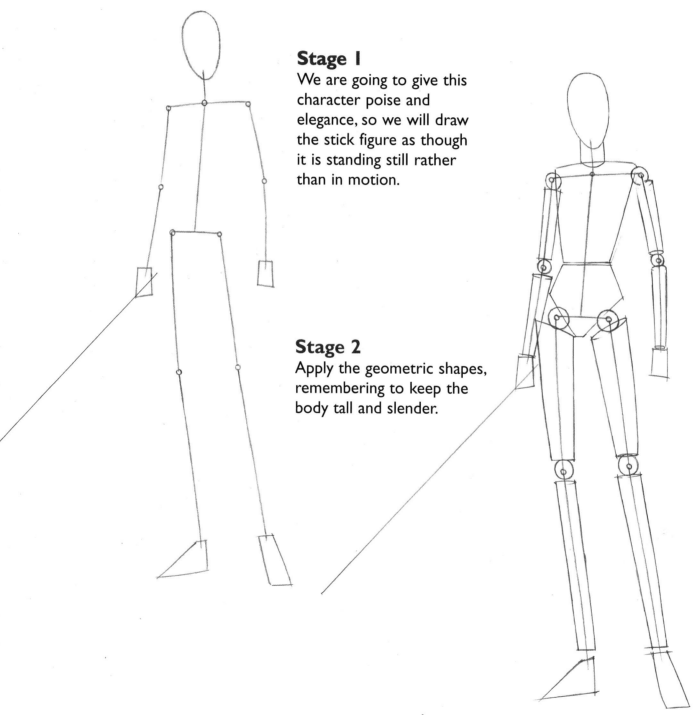

Stage 1
We are going to give this character poise and elegance, so we will draw the stick figure as though it is standing still rather than in motion.

Stage 2
Apply the geometric shapes, remembering to keep the body tall and slender.

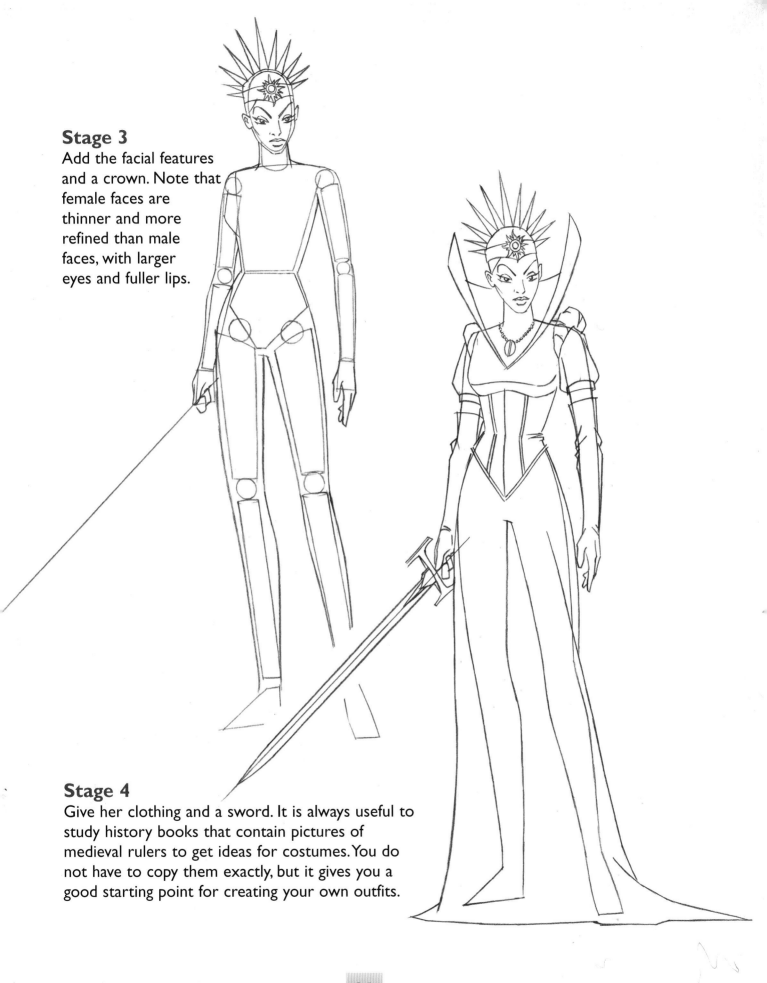

Stage 3

Add the facial features and a crown. Note that female faces are thinner and more refined than male faces, with larger eyes and fuller lips.

Stage 4

Give her clothing and a sword. It is always useful to study history books that contain pictures of medieval rulers to get ideas for costumes. You do not have to copy them exactly, but it gives you a good starting point for creating your own outfits.

Stage 5

Add further details to the costume, such as delicate lace on the bodice and folds in the gown. Note that the decoration on this sword distinguishes it from an everyday battle weapon.

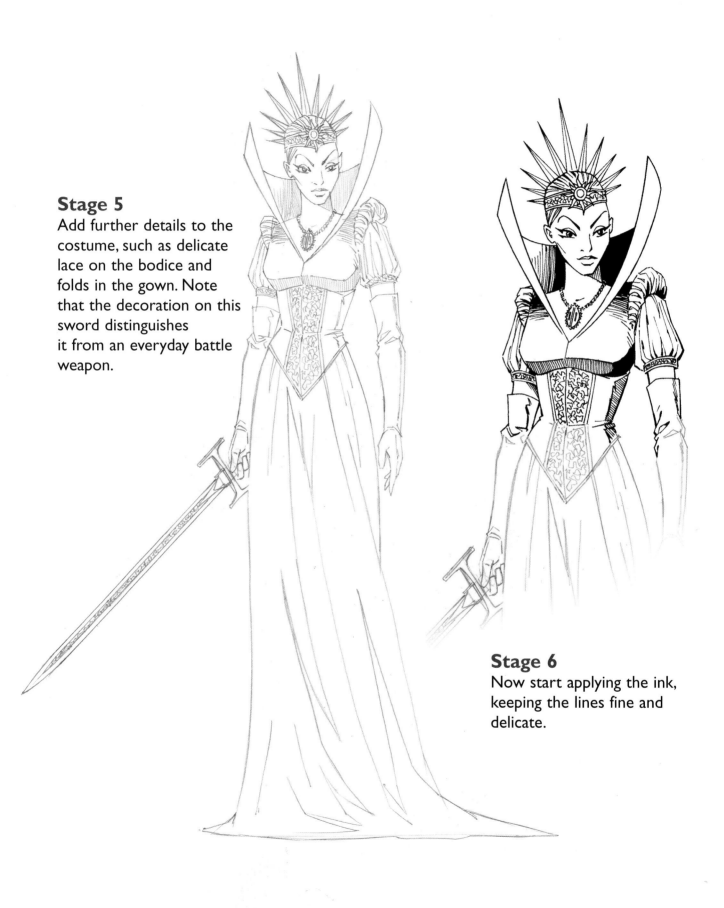

Stage 6

Now start applying the ink, keeping the lines fine and delicate.

Stage 7

The solid shadow of her high collar has helped define her face. However, the overall look is still light.

Stage 8

Finally, apply color, if you wish to. Using bright, warm yellows and golds helps establish this character as a force for good.

Evil Queen

This queen's looks also reflect her personality. She is clearly a ruthless woman who will stop at nothing in her quest for power over everybody and everything. She is prepared to use every trick in the book to get what she desires.

Stage 1

We want to show our queen as a figure who strikes fear in the hearts of her subjects. Therefore, we will use a more dynamic pose for the stick figure than we did for the good queen. To add to the effect, we will include a little evil sidekick at her feet.

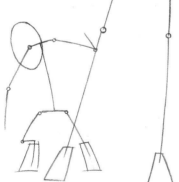

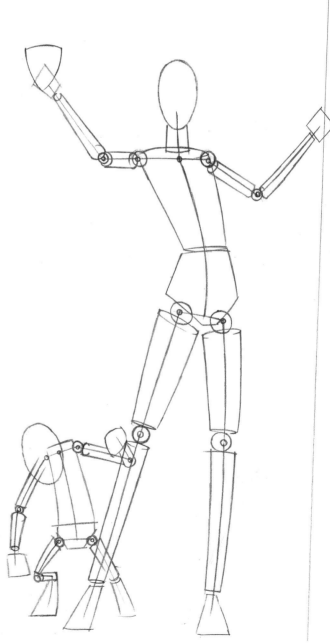

Stage 2

Use long cylinders for the queen's limbs when adding the geometric shapes and short ones to create a stunted frame for her little helper.

Stage 3

Although the facial features are attractive, they also have a certain cruelty. Have as much fun as you like creating an ugly face for her pet. At this stage we can add the outer body form.

Stage 4

Now erase the geometric shapes and add in the outline of her costume. Note how it gives her the appearance of a demon or some creature of the night.

Stage 5
The horned headdress reinforces the aura of evil that surrounds this queen. Place a steaming goblet of evil potion in one hand and a mystical staff, complete with magic crystal, in the other.

Stage 6
Now finish off the pencil sketch by adding a few final details and some shading. At this stage we decide that most of her costume will be solid black in the final drawing.

Stage 7
Now begin to apply the ink. Create shading by drawing closely spaced parallel lines, known as crosshatching.

Stage 8
Note that the inking is heavier here than on earlier drawings. There are large areas of solid black, leaving very little detail in the costume or the drawing as a whole. This simple use of solid black adds greatly to the power of the image.

Stage 9

The use of purple clearly defines this queen as evil. Note the pale tone of her skin—she is probably allergic to daylight! Green is always a good choice for pesky-looking demons.

Glossary

anatomy (uh-NA-tuh-mee) The physical structure of a human or other organism.

aura (OR-uh) A distinctive impression created by somebody or something.

bodice (BAH-dus) The part of a woman's dress that covers the upper body.

broadsword (BROD-sord) A sword with a wide, flat blade, designed for cutting rather than thrusting.

contrast (KAHN-trast) An effect created by placing different colors or shades next to each other.

corrupt (kuh-RUPT) Make someone or something become immoral or dishonest.

crosshatching (KROS-hach-ing) Parallel or intersecting lines drawn across part of a drawing, usually diagonally, to give the effect of shadow.

cylinder (SIH-len-der) A shape with straight sides and circular ends of equal size.

dynamic (dy-NA-mik) Full of energy.

facial (FAY-shul) Of the face.

functional (FUNGK-shnul) Having a practical purpose.

geometric shape (jee-uh-MEH-trik SHAYP) A simple shape, such as a cube, sphere, or cylinder.

gouache (GWAHSH) A mixture of non-transparent watercolor paint and gum.

mechanical pencil (mih-KA-nih-kul PENT-sul) A pencil with replaceable lead that may be advanced as needed.

medieval (mee-DEE-vul) Relating to the Middle Ages in Europe (approximately A.D. 1000 to 1500).

mystical (MIS-tih-kul) Something with supernatural or spiritual significance or power.

oppress (uh-PRES) To subject a people to harsh rule.

perspective (per-SPEK-tiv) In drawing, changing the relative size and appearance of objects to allow for the effects of distance.

poise (POYZ) Calm and self-assured dignity.

potion (POH-shun) A drink with magical powers.

refined (rih-FYND) Graceful and elegant.

sable brush (SAY-bul BRUSH) An artist's brush made with the hairs of a sable, a small mammal from northern Asia.

sphere (SFEER) An object shaped like a ball.

stick figure (STIK FIH-gyur) A simple drawing of a person with single lines for the body, arms, and legs.

stunted (STUNT-ed) Something of restricted growth.

watercolor (WO-ter-kuh-ler) Paint made by mixing pigments with water.

Further Reading

Books

Drawing and Painting Fantasy Figures: From the Imagination to the Page by Finlay Cowan (David and Charles, 2004)

Draw Medieval Fantasies by Damon J. Reinagle (Peel Productions, 1995)

How to Draw Fantasy Characters by Christopher Hart (Watson-Guptill Publications, 1999)

How to Draw Wizards, Dragons and other Magical Creatures by Barbara Soloff Levy (Dover Publications, 2004)

Kids Draw Knights, Kings, Queens and Dragons by Christopher Hart (Watson-Guptill Publications, 2001)

Web Sites

Due to the changing nature of Internet links, PowerKids Press has developed an online list of Web sites related to the subject of this book. This site is updated regularly. Please use this link to access the list: www.powerkidslinks.com/dfa/kings/

Index